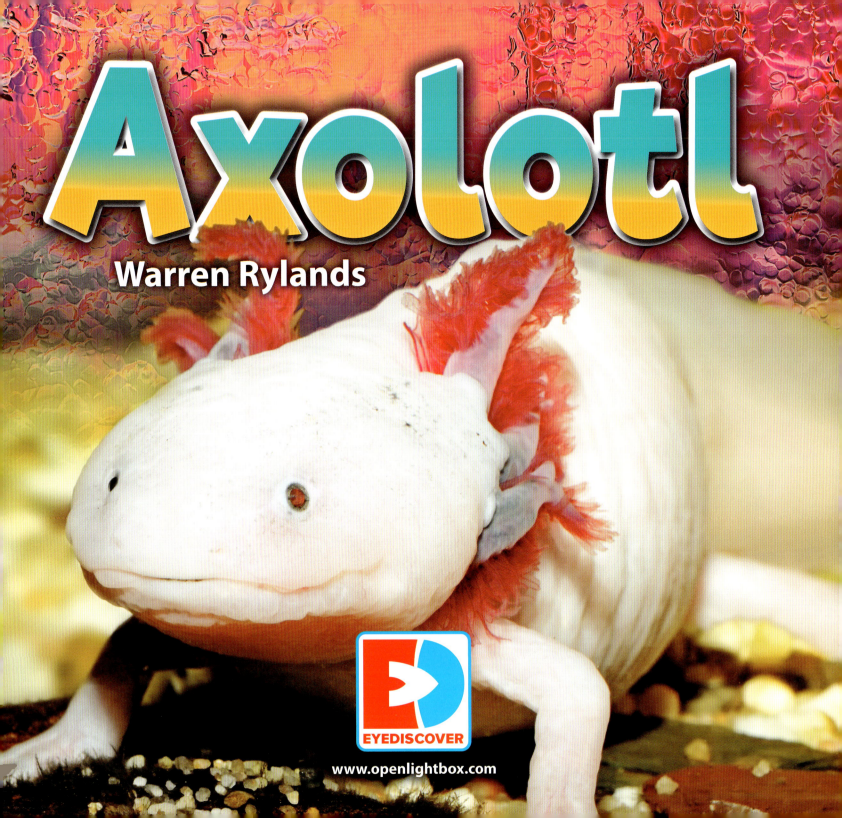

Go to www.openlightbox.com and enter this book's unique code.

BOOK CODE
AVD62982

EYEDISCOVER brings you optic readalongs that support active learning.

Published by Lightbox Learning Inc.
276 5th Avenue, Suite 704 #917
New York, NY 10001
Website: www.openlightbox.com

Copyright ©2024 Lightbox Learning Inc.
All rights reserved. No part of this publication may be reproduced, stored in a retrieval system, or transmitted in any form or by any means, electronic, mechanical, photocopying, recording, or otherwise, without the prior written permission of the publisher.

Library of Congress Control Number: 2023947047

ISBN 978-1-7911-5932-0 (hardcover)

Printed in Guangzhou, China
2 3 4 5 6 7 8 9 0 28 27 26 25 24

022024
240209

Project Coordinator: Priyanka Das
Art Director: Terry Paulhus
Layout: Jean Marie Faye Rodriguez

The publisher acknowledges Alamy, Getty Images, and Shutterstock as the primary image suppliers for this title.

2

EYEDISCOVER provides enriched content, optimized for tablet use, that supplements and complements this book. EYEDISCOVER books strive to create inspired learning and engage young minds in a total learning experience.

Watch
Video content brings each page to life.

Browse
Thumbnails make navigation simple.

Read
Follow along with text on the screen.

Listen
Hear each page read aloud.

Your EYEDISCOVER Optic Readalongs come alive with...

Audio
Listen to the entire book read aloud.

Video
High resolution videos turn each spread into an optic readalong.

OPTIMIZED FOR
☑ **TABLETS**
☑ **WHITEBOARDS**
☑ **COMPUTERS**
☑ **AND MUCH MORE!**

This title is part of our EyeDiscover digital subscription

1-Year EyeDiscover Subscription
ISBN 978-1-4896-8346-5

Access all EyeDiscover titles with our digital subscription. Sign up for a FREE trial at **www.openlightbox.com/trial**

The digital components of this book are guaranteed to stay active for at least five years from the date of publication.

Axolotl

In this book, you will learn about

- what it is
- where it lives
- how it looks

and much more!

4

Axolotls are Mexican salamanders. The word *axolotl* sounds like "ax-uh-lah-tuhl."

Axolotls are also called "Mexican walking fish." However, they are not fish.

6

7

Axolotls are amphibians. Unlike most amphibians, they spend their whole lives underwater.

In nature, axolotls can only be found in and around Lake Xochimilco in Mexico City.

Axolotls eat worms, insects, and small fish.

14

Axolotls come in many colors. In nature, they are usually dark brown, gray, or green.

Pet axolotls are often light in color. Many have white bodies and pink gills.

An axolotl can live up to 15 years.

21

AXOLOTLS BY THE NUMBERS

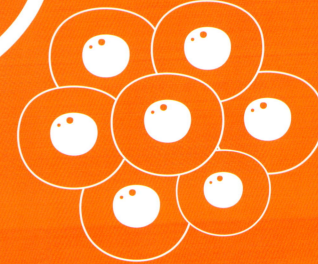

Axolotls grow to be about **10 inches** (25 centimeters) in length.

FEMALE axolotls can **LAY** up to **1,000 EGGS** at a time.

In **nature**, axolotls live for about **5 or 6 years**.

Axolotls have been a **popular** part of the *Minecraft* video game since **2021**.

About **1 million** axolotls are kept as **pets** or found in **aquariums** and **laboratories**.

There are **FEWER THAN 1,000** axolotls left in **LAKE XOCHIMILCO**.

23

KEY WORDS

Research has shown that as much as 65 percent of all written material published in English is made up of 300 words. These 300 words cannot be taught using pictures or learned by sounding them out. They must be recognized by sight. This book contains 36 common sight words to help young readers improve their reading fluency and comprehension. This book also teaches young readers several important content words, such as proper nouns. These words are paired with pictures to aid in learning and improve understanding.

Page	Sight Words First Appearance
5	are, like, sounds, the, word
6	also, not, they
9	lives, most, their
10	and, around, be, can, city, found, in, only
12	eat, small
15	almost, an, any, it, part
16	come, many, or
19	have, light, often, white
20	to, up, years

Page	Content Words First Appearance
5	axolotls, salamanders
6	fish
9	amphibians
10	Lake Xochimilco, Mexico City, nature
12	insects, worms
16	brown, colors, gray, green
19	bodies, gills

Watch Video content brings each page to life.

Browse Thumbnails make navigation simple.

Read Follow along with text on the screen.

Listen Hear each page read aloud.

EYEDISCOVER

Go to www.openlightbox.com and enter this book's unique code.

BOOK CODE
AVD62982